A long time ago, two children lived near a big forest. The boy's name was Hansel. His sister's name was Gretel.

The children's father, Hans, was a woodcutter. He cut down trees in the forest and made beautiful toys and furniture, bowls and boxes. He sold them in the market. He worked very hard. Hansel and Gretel helped their mother, Greta, in the house and garden. They were poor but they were happy.

One day Greta died. 'Oh dear!' said Hans. 'Now my children have no mother!' He was very sad.

a woodcutter

One day Hans met a woman in the market. Her name was Anna. After a short time, Hans asked Anna, 'Will you marry me?'

'Yes!' answered Anna.

Soon they were married.

'This is your new mother,' said Hans to the children.

Anna was nice to Hansel and Gretel when Hans was at home, but she often hit them when Hans was at work. They tried to tell Hans but he did not want to listen to them. Hansel and Gretel were very sad.

marry / married   hit

One night, the children were in bed. They heard Anna's angry voice in the kitchen.

'They're bad, naughty children,' she said. 'And we haven't got enough food for them to eat. Hans, you must leave them in the middle of the forest.'

'No, I can't! They are my children,' said Hans.

Anna cried and shouted, 'But I don't like them!'

Hans was tired. 'Oh, all right,' he said. 'I'll leave them in the forest tomorrow. Now, be quiet. I want to sleep.'

leave

1. Look at the pictures. Write the right words. What is the word in the red box? Read it.

2. What will happen next? Tick one sentence.

   a) Hans will leave the children in the forest.

   b) Hans will leave the children in the forest, but they will come home again.

   c) Hans will leave Anna in the forest.

   d) Anna will leave the children in the forest.

Hansel and Gretel were very afraid. Then Hansel had a clever idea. The next morning, he got up at five o'clock and went outside. He collected a lot of small white stones and put them in his pocket. Then he went back to bed.

'Wake up, children!' called Anna at seven o'clock. 'You're going to go to the forest with your father today.'

The children followed their father into the big forest. Every few minutes, Hansel took a stone out of his pocket and dropped it on the ground.

a pocket

They walked and walked. Now they were in the middle of the forest. Hans said, 'Pick some beautiful flowers for Anna. I'm going to cut down some trees. I'll come back soon.' Then he went away.

'Now we're lost!' said Gretel.

'No, we aren't,' said Hansel. 'Look! I dropped a white stone every few minutes. We can follow them, and we'll find our house.'

The children followed the stones through the big, dark forest. Soon they were at home again. Anna was very angry when she saw them.

went away

That night, Anna shouted at Hans again.

The next morning, Hansel got up at five o'clock. He wanted to find some more white stones but the door was locked. He saw some bread on the table so he put some in his pocket.

Hans took the children into the forest again. Every few minutes Hansel dropped a small piece of bread on the ground. Soon Hans and the children were in the middle of the forest. Then Hans went away. Hansel looked at the ground. There was no bread. 'Some birds ate the bread,' shouted Gretel. The children were lost!

a small piece

Puzzles

Look at the pictures. Write the missing words.

Hans took Hansel and a) _____ into the middle of

the b) _____. Hansel had a lot of small white

c) _____ in his d) _____. He

e) _____ them on the ground. The children

f) _____ the stones and went home. The

next morning the g) _____ was locked. Hansel

put some h) _____ in his pocket. He dropped small

pieces on the ground but some i) _____

ate them. Now the j) _____ were lost!

Soon the children saw a beautiful house. The walls were made of cake. The roof was made of chocolate. The door and windows were made of biscuits and sweets. The door opened. An old woman came out.

'Come inside,' she said.

Hansel and Gretel followed her into the house. The old woman locked the door. She pushed Hansel into a cage and locked it with a big black key. 'I'm going to cook you and eat you, but you aren't fat enough yet!' she said. She looked at Gretel. 'And you can do all the work in the house.'

The old woman gave Hansel lots of good food, for example, chicken, meat, cheese and milk. Every day she said, 'Are you fat enough to eat yet? Let me feel your finger.' But Hansel always gave her a chicken bone to feel.

'You're too thin,' said the old woman, and she gave him some more food.

One morning the old woman became angry.

'Why aren't you fat yet?' she shouted. 'I'm very hungry. I'm going to cook you today!'

She shouted to Gretel, 'Go and fetch some wood and make a fire under the oven.'

wood

an oven

Gretel wanted to run away but she also wanted to help Hansel. So she went back to the old woman's house with some wood. She made a fire under the oven.

'Now,' said the old woman, 'is the oven hot enough?'

'I don't know,' said Gretel.

'Open the oven door and feel inside,' said the old woman.

'How?' asked Gretel.

'Let me show you,' said the old woman. She opened the door of the oven and put her head inside.

run away

Puzzles

The pictures are in the right order. Write the letters in the right boxes to tell the story.

☐	'Is the oven hot enough?' the old woman asked Gretel.
☐	There was a big oven in the old woman's kitchen.
☐	'I don't know,' said Gretel.
☐	The old woman opened the door of the oven.
☐	Gretel made a big fire under the oven.
☐	'I'm going to cook you today!' shouted the old woman.
☐	The old woman put her head inside the oven.
a	One day the old woman felt Hansel's chicken bone and became angry. 'Why aren't you fat yet?' she shouted.
☐	'Fetch some wood!' said the old woman to Gretel.

Quickly, Gretel pushed the old woman into the oven. The key of the cage fell out of her pocket. Gretel closed the door of the oven.

Gretel picked up the key. She opened the cage quickly. 'Thank you!' said Hansel. 'You're very clever.'

Then Hansel saw a big box under the table. They opened it and found a lot of gold inside. 'Let's go home and give the gold to Dad!' said Hansel.

fell out

Hansel put the gold in a big bag. He carried the bag on his shoulder. Then they ran out of the old woman's house and walked through the forest. The sun was in the sky. There was light in the forest so Hansel and Gretel were not afraid. They walked and walked, then they met a woodcutter.

'Can you help us, please?' they asked. 'We're lost.'

The woodcutter walked through the forest with them and
helped them to find their house.

Hans was in the garden. He looked sad. He saw the children and shouted, 'Hansel! Gretel!' He ran to them and put his arms round them.

'Where's Anna?' asked Gretel.

'Anna died last week,' said Hans.

Hansel and Gretel told their father about the old woman and her house, the cage, the bone and the big oven. Then they opened the bag and showed Hans the gold. 'We'll never be poor again!' said Hansel.

Puzzles

Gretel is telling her friend about the old woman. Write the missing words in the blanks for her.

I a) _____ (push) the old woman into the oven. The key of the cage b) _____ (fall) out of her pocket. I c) _____ (open) the cage and Hansel d) _____ (come) out. We e) _____ (find) a box of gold. We f) _____ (run) out of the old woman's house. We g) _____ (walk) through the forest and h) _____ (meet) a woodcutter. He i) _____ (help) us to find our house. Father j) _____ (see) us and k) _____ (run) to us. He l) _____ (put) his arms round us. We m) _____ (give) him the gold. He n) _____ (be) very happy.

Forests

A forest is a large piece of land with a lot of trees. There are different kinds of forests all over the world.

In some places there are different seasons in a year. The trees in the forests in these places usually have large leaves. They use sunlight and water to make food for the tree in the summer. In the autumn, the green leaves change to yellow, orange, red or brown and fall off the trees. In the winter the trees are bare. Then, in the spring, new leaves grow again.

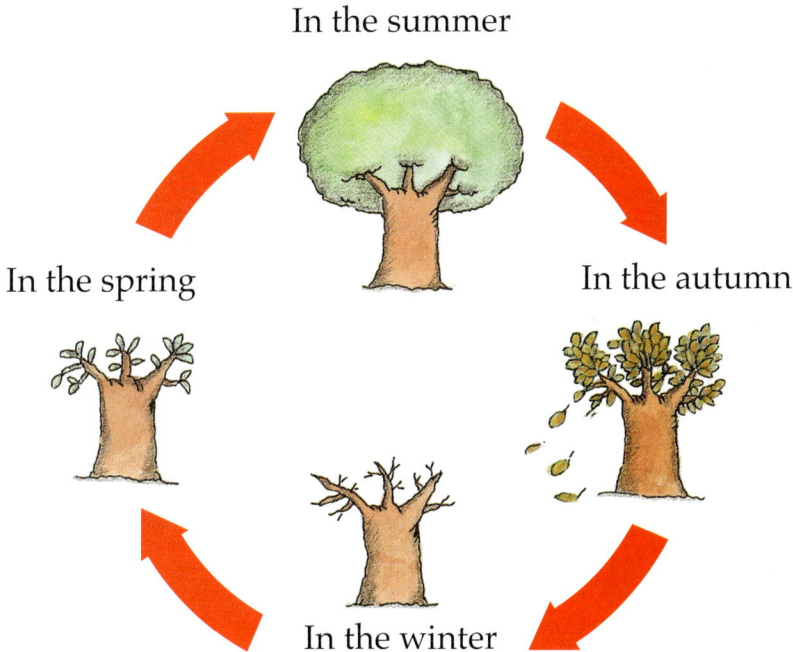

In the summer

In the spring

In the autumn

In the winter

fall off

bare

In some forests trees are never bare. Leaves do not fall off the trees every year. The trees are always green so we call these forests evergreen forests. These forests are in cold countries with long winters and short summers. Trees in these forests do not need much sunlight. They have needle-shaped leaves.

SIBERIA

The largest evergreen forest is in Siberia. It is 11 million square kilometres.

needle-shaped leaves

Some forests are in hot, wet places near the equator. These places have no summer or winter. It is hot all the time. There is always a lot of sunlight and a lot of rain so people call these forests rain forests.

The largest rain forest in the world is in South America. It is 6.5 million square kilometres.

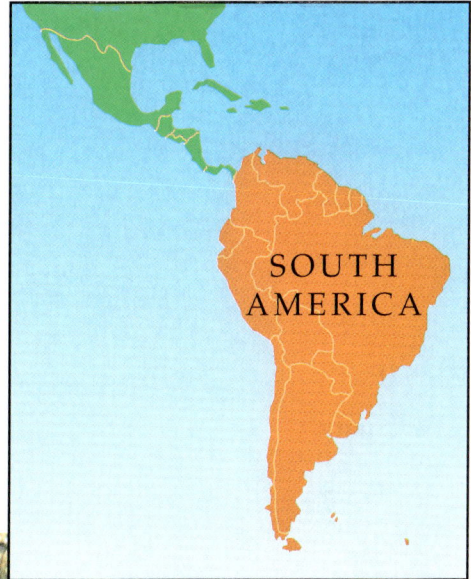

SOUTH
AMERICA

There are many, many trees and flowers in a rain forest. Many beautiful animals and insects live there, for example, frogs, orang-utans, monkeys, snakes and lizards. There are thousands of birds, too. A rain forest is a very noisy place!

Puzzles

1. Find these words in the word square.

leaves
green
long
bare
birds
trees
winter
summer
lizards
snakes
sunlight
rain forest

L	O	N	G	R	E	E	N	P	S
I	R	M	R	I	N	S	E	C	T
Z	W	E	O	B	I	R	D	S	O
A	N	I	U	J	A	D	R	O	P
R	A	I	N	F	O	R	E	S	T
D	N	C	D	T	R	K	E	N	R
S	I	I	M	L	E	V	E	A	E
Y	M	N	P	L	A	R	E	K	E
S	U	M	M	E	R	Y	C	E	S
S	U	N	L	I	G	H	T	S	D

2. Match the two parts of these sentences.

a) The largest rain forest in the world is • • a lot of trees.

b) A forest is a large piece of land with • • in cold countries.

c) Evergreen forests are • • in South America.

d) Rain forests are in hot, wet places • • in the winter.

e) In some forests the trees are bare • • near the equator.

20

People live in rain forests, too. They know a lot about animals and plants. They collect fruit, roots, nuts and other parts of plants to eat. They also catch animals for food. Some people make medicines from plants.

Some people cut down the trees to make farms but they do not plant any new trees. Many birds, animals and insects die because they have nowhere to live.

Some people do not live in rain forests but they go to rain forests to cut down the trees and sell the wood to make money.

nuts

medicines

plant

Rain forests are very important because many things come from them, for example, wood, bananas, coffee and nuts. But our forests are in danger because people are cutting down too many trees every year.

When there are no more trees in a forest and the animals eat the grass and the small plants, the forest becomes a desert.

a desert

Deserts

This is a desert. Deserts are very dry places. There are mountains, rocks and sand in deserts. Deserts get very little rain. There are deserts in hot places like Africa and in places like the northern part of China, too. It is very hot during the day and very cold at night in a desert.

There are plants in deserts. Most plants in deserts need very little water to grow. Cacti grow in deserts. They keep water in their thick stems. They have no leaves but tiny spines so they do not lose water easily.

cacti

spines

Animals and insects live in deserts, too. Some of them sleep during the day because it is too hot, and come out to find food at night.

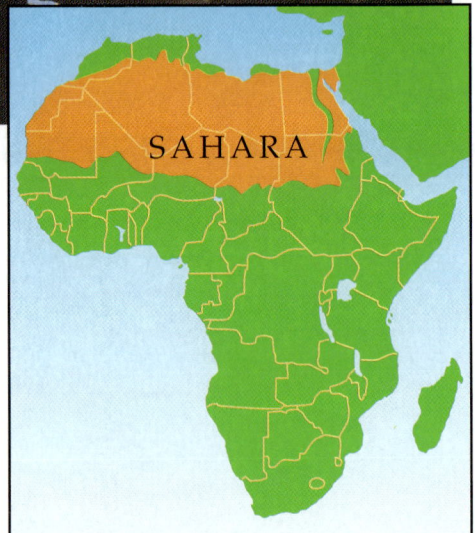

SAHARA

Camels are the largest animals in deserts. They have thick fur to keep them cool during the day and warm at night.

The Sahara is the largest desert in the world. It is in many countries in Africa.

Puzzles

Write the right words in the blanks and in the puzzle.

a) Some people cut down trees and sell the wood for _____.

b) Rain forests are in danger because people are cutting down too many _____.

c) A desert is a very _____ place.

d) Cacti do not have any leaves. They have _____.

e) _____ are the largest animals in deserts.

f) Deserts get very little _____.

g) People in rain forests catch _____ for food.

h) Some animals in deserts _____ during the day and come out to find food at night.

i) Cacti keep water in their _____.

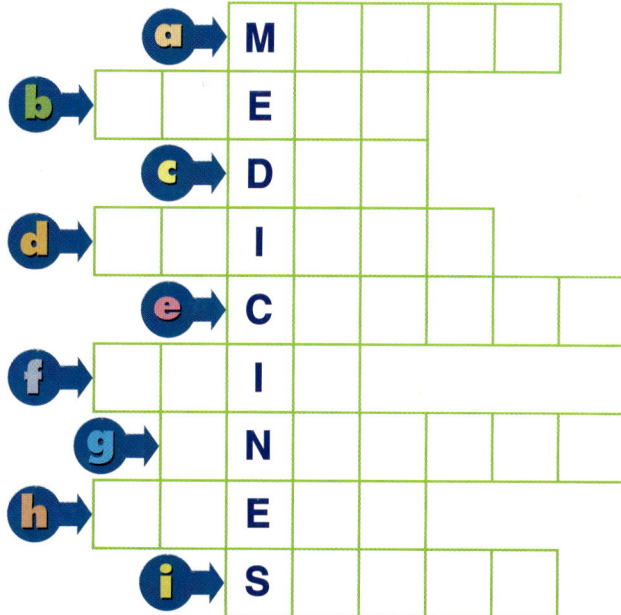

a → M
b → E
c → D
d → I
e → C
f → I
g → N
h → E
i → S

Trees

Trees are very important. They are the homes of many birds and animals. They give us food, for example, fruit and nuts. People make different things from trees, for example, paper.

How do you find out the age of a tree? Every year the tree grows a little and a ring grows round the trunk of the tree. When people cut down the tree, you can count the number of rings in the trunk to tell the age of the tree. In 1964 a woodcutter cut down a tree and counted 4,900 rings inside the tree!

Today the tallest tree in the world is a redwood tree in the United States of America. It is 113 metres tall.

The smallest trees in the world do not grow in forests. They are bonsai trees. Some bonsai trees are very old, and all bonsai trees are very small. Their leaves and fruit are small, too.

People plant bonsai trees in very small trays and do not give them much water. The trees do not die, but they grow very slowly.

trays

27

Make a Sweet House!

This little house is a beautiful birthday cake. You need:

some jam

two large square cakes

sweets of different colours

a large rectangular biscuit

a large bar of chocolate

1 Break the bar of chocolate into small pieces. Keep the foil.

2 Put the pieces in a bowl, and put the bowl in hot water to melt the chocolate.

3 Cut one cake into halves. Put some jam on one half and put the other half on top. This is your house.

4 Cut the other cake into two triangles. Stick them together with jam. This is the roof. Put some jam on the top of the house. Put the roof on top of the house.

5 Put melted chocolate all over your house and make it smooth.

6 Cut the foil from the chocolate into squares and stick it onto the walls. These are the windows.

7 Stick the large biscuit onto the house. This is the door.

8 Make your house look beautiful with the sweets.

Questions

Page 1
a) Where did the family live?
b) What was the children's father?
c) Were they rich?

Page 2
a) Where did Hans meet Anna?
b) Was Anna always nice to Hansel and Gretel?
c) Did Hans listen to the children?

Page 3
a) Where were the children?
b) Where were Anna and Hans?
c) What did Anna want Hans to do?

Page 5
a) Hansel got up at **five** / **six** / **seven** o'clock in the morning.
b) Hansel collected a lot of **flowers** / **sticks** / **stones**.

Page 6
True or *false*?
a) Hans left Hansel and Gretel in the middle of the forest.
b) Hansel and Gretel followed the stones to go home.
c) Anna was very happy to see Hansel and Gretel.

Page 7
a) What did Hansel put in his pocket?
b) What did Hansel do in the forest?
c) Why were Hansel and Gretel lost?

Page 9
a) The roof of the house was made of _____.
b) The door and windows were made of _____.
c) The old woman pushed Hansel into a _____.

Page 10 a) What did the old woman feel?

             b) What did the old woman want Gretel to do?

Page 11 a) Did Gretel go back to the old woman's house?

             b) Did Gretel open the oven and feel inside?

             c) Who put her head inside the oven?

Page 13 a) What did Gretel do to the old woman?

             b) What did Hansel and Gretel find under the table?

Page 14 a) Where did Hansel put the gold?

             b) Were Hansel and Gretel afraid?

             c) Who helped them to find their house?

Page 15 Who said these?

             a) 'Hansel! Gretel!'

             b) 'Where's Anna?'

             c) 'We'll never be poor again!'

Page 17 a) A _____ is a large piece of land with lots of trees.

             b) Leaves use _____ and water to make food for the tree.

Page 18 *True* or *false*?

             a) All trees are bare in the winter.

             b) Many trees in cold countries have needle-shaped leaves.

             c) The largest evergreen forest is in Siberia.

Page 19 a) Are there any rain forests in cold, dry places?

             b) Where is the largest rain forest in the world?

             c) Why is a rain forest a noisy place?

Page 21   a) Do people live in rain forests?

              b) Why do birds, animals and insects die?

Page 22   a) Why are forests in danger?

              b) What happens when there are no more trees in a forest?

Page 23   a) Deserts are very **dry** / **wet** places.

              b) Cacti keep water in their **spines** / **stems**.

              c) Most plants in deserts need **a lot of** / **very little** water to grow.

Page 24   a) Why do some animals and insects in deserts sleep during the day?

              b) What keeps camels warm at night?

              c) Where is the largest desert in the world?

Page 26   a) How do you tell the age of a tree?

              b) How many rings does a tree grow every year?

Page 27   a) How tall is the tallest tree in the world?

              b) What do we call the smallest trees in the world?

Page 28   a) How many different things do you need to make the cake?

              b) How do you melt the chocolate?

Page 29   a) What do you use to make the windows?

              b) What do you use to make the door?